PROCUREMENT METHODS
METHODS

EFFECTIVE TECHNIQUES

PROCUREMENT METHODS

EFFECTIVE TECHNIQUES

Reference Guide for Procurement Professionals

By Lourdes Coss, MPA, CPPO

I dedicate this book to my wonderful daughter Laika with all of my love. Her love and support keeps me moving forward. I also dedicate this book to my parents, Lolin and Manuel, and my sisters, Maritza and Doris, for they have always believed in me and love me unconditionally.

"Understanding the logic for selecting the process and putting the solicitation document together is half the battle.

Learn the logic and the rest is practice!"

—Lourdes Coss

TABLE OF CONTENTS

ACKNOWLEDGMENTS

First I want to thank God for He gives me strength and always shows me the way.

I want to express my sincere appreciation to my friends Jennifer and Elvia. They encouraged me to share my experience and knowledge with others, especially the new generation of procurement professionals. Their pep talks moved me to start writing. My gratitude also goes to my friends Adriana, Julie, and Calvin for believing in me and encouraging me to expand my horizons.

INTRODUCTION

Procurement: an art or a science? Experienced procurement professionals will probably say that it is both. After more than 25 years in this profession, I most definitely agree. These two dimensions offer procurement professionals the opportunity to provide creative solutions using consistent methods. A quest for balance between these two dimensions keeps the job interesting and engaging.

Most procurement professionals, myself included, entered the profession by chance. Those of us who discovered this somewhat hidden treasure in the midst of a multitude of tasks have stayed and cultivated a skillset that balances the art and science that in some way has helped weave the fabric of procurement as we know it today.

Let's briefly review the skillset required. I know that many assume that anyone can do procurement regardless of skills and experience. Why not? Everyone buys something at one time or another! While buying is part of procurement, professional procurement is more than just buying. Professional procurement also requires research, analysis, communication skills, public speaking skills, leadership skills, problem solving skills, the ability to build relationships, and creative thinking while upholding high ethical standards in a highly regulated environment. The individual skills required are not really unique, processes can be learned on the job, and techniques can be learned over time. It is interesting, however, that the absence of skills to support both procurement dimensions may result in either rigid processes with minimum to no creativity for problem solving or conversely the lack of consistent processes and order.

Many of us have worked incessantly to elevate the quality of procurement and offer organizations the value it didn't know it could offer. A high performing procurement team can help organizations achieve their goals whether financial, socio-economic, operational, or all of the above. Those organizations that have recognized its value generally enjoy an enviable level of excellence that may be unattainable by others, perhaps because they have not recognized its potential. Achieving the title of "high performing procurement organization" offering a level of excellence admired by others requires the alignment of many factors and strategies. One of the most important factors in achieving that level of excellence lies in the hands of the team of procurement professionals in the organization.

With some exceptions, most government procurement organizations may not be considered high performing organizations. This is due in part to the absence or limitations of resources like adequate staffing, tools, and training supported by a culture that embraces the value of procurement and its potential. This is simply a reality of life and there's no point dwelling on it. This book is focused on providing a simple tool or guide to managers and procurement staff to facilitate the training process for the next generation of procurement professionals. It is intended to fill the gap left by the limitation of resources that forces agencies to use the training method referred to as "sink or swim." As many of us know, this dreaded method is based on trial and error. The chance and hope that we get it right so that we can move on to the next request! This method, while it may appear to require less supervisor training time, makes resources seem even more limited. Why? The reason is simple; one has to do it again if it doesn't work the first time.

I often hear from my colleagues that it is hard to find qualified candidates to fill their positions, including entry-level positions. I shared this opinion as I dealt with limited staffing levels and no time to train someone who didn't walk in the door knowing the different application of procurement methods, part of the basics in procurement. Since the training budgets are scarce and staffing levels are generally insufficient for the demand, it is important to hire staff that has had some hands-on training in another organization. It is, therefore, necessary to hire, even at the entry-level, staff with some experience and the qualifications to hit the ground running. Otherwise, it puts a tremendous pressure on managers, as they are the ones left with the responsibility to train newcomers and yet try to keep their heads above water with all of the other demands.

With many of the procurement professionals either retiring or close to retirement, coupled with resource limitations, there is a good chance that the knowledge acquired throughout the years in the profession, even if by trial and error, may leave the organizations as we depart. With a shrinking pool of trained professionals and insufficient time for knowledge transfer, new procurement professionals will be required to make the same mistakes we made as we developed into leaders of this profession. We might be shooting ourselves in the foot by not investing the time to train this next generation. Let's face it, this next generation of procurement professionals will be influencing or making decisions that will impact taxpayers, including the retired population.

This book *Procurement Methods: Effective Techniques* is intended to assist managers in the training process. It is a tool that provides basic guidance to new procurement professionals regarding the selection and use of the three basic competitive procurement methods with the goal of having new staff work independently sooner, while managers can focus on agency-specific requirements training. Providing written guidance will inject consistency in the training process and help new team members become productive contributors more quickly. While I was fortunate to work with great leaders early in my career, it would have been nice to have a written guide so that I could avoid some of my own mistakes along the way.

This book *Procurement Methods: Effective Techniques* is organized by method of procurement. In this book I break down the key components of the procurement document for each basic method and explain the rationale that goes into putting the solicitation document together. You will be able to apply the techniques to make the procurement process effective. I provide examples, describe the process for developing the procurement documents, and clarify the terminology. It should be noted that agencies often use methods that are derivatives of the methods discussed; therefore, understanding the objective of the method and how its parts complement each other will help make the adaptations necessary when using one of the variations of the procurement methods. I included the information that I used over the years to train staff on these methods. I found that this information is generally what procurement professionals need to get the basics right as it relates to the application of the different methods of procurement. This reference guide can be part of the welcome package of reading material for new procurement staff and the training assistance that managers need.

PROCUREMENT METHODS

METHODS

EFFECTIVE TECHNIQUES

CHAPTER I
Bids or Competitive (Sealed) Bids

Myth: Low bid equals lowest quality. The bid process is a competitive procurement method that helps identify the lowest responsive and responsible bidder. This means that the contract is awarded to the lowest bidder whose bid meets the requirements of the bid document and whose qualifications meet the minimum requirements specified.

The bid or competitive sealed bid is the "go to" method for goods and work services. It saves time, as no evaluation committee is required after bids are received. This method can be very effective and efficient when applied correctly. The bid review process can be divided into three steps: responsiveness, price, and responsibility review. These are the same three areas as the RFP, but the review of price and qualifications is done differently.

Many shy away from this method due to their belief that the low bidder, regardless of qualifications, must be awarded the contract. This is not the case, as bids must first be responsive before the ascending pricing hierarchy is established. Once the price stacking is done (including correct arithmetic), responsibility of the apparent lowest bidder must be determined. The low bidder must also be deemed responsible (to have met all of the requirements and qualifications to perform the services or provide the goods) before it is awarded a contract. Unlike the RFP, the price is considered before the qualifications, and price is heavily weighted.

The use of the right terminology will help avoid confusion regarding how the steps are handled. For example, those submitting a response to the Invitation for Bid (IFB) or Invitation to Bid (ITB) are referred to as "bidders" and their response is referred to as "bid."

OBJECTIVE AND APPLICATION

Objective

The objective of the bid process is to obtain the lowest price based on a responsive bid submitted by a responsible bidder.

Application

This method is generally more appropriate for the procurement of commodities, equipment, work services, or construction. These are goods and services that can be specified and any tolerances identified. Generally, the services or goods are essentially the same regardless of the vendor.

ITB OR IFB DEVELOPMENT

Invitations for bid offer the greatest opportunity to standardize documents, although, some customization may still be necessary to accommodate creative ideas on certain projects. Parts of the bid that are generally standardized include but are not limited to the instructions to bidders, general terms and conditions applicable to the organization, forms and specific agency requirements, offer and acceptance section, and price or proposal page format. I will focus on key areas where some customization may be required. These include: the summary page, specifications, requirements and/or qualifications of a supplier or contractor, the basis of award, and the price proposal details.

Project Summary

The project summary provides a snapshot of the project and requirements. Some but not all agencies include this summary page. The summary page will generally include the name of the project; a brief description of the scope in no more than two to three sentences; the due date, time and place for bid submission; buyer contact information; bid deposit, bid bond, and/or bonding requirements; date, time, and location of the pre-bid conference; due date for the submission of questions, where and to whom questions are to be submitted; and anything else that the agency wishes to highlight. This one-page summary is helpful to both the bidder and the agency issuing the bid.

Specifications

The specifications must be clear and shall articulate what is sought, any tolerances or ranges, allowable alternates or substitutions, and any standards that must be met, as applicable. For the most part, the end user will provide the detailed specifications. An example of specifications may consist of a list of items indicating a specific grade, quality standard, quantity, color, size, frequency of service, and any other information that may be applicable or necessary for bidders to provide pricing. There is more detailed information on the scope or item description in a bid when compared to the other methods of procurement. There is a specific need and the agency can articulate what it is.

> **Example Supplies: Paper goods**
> -Napkins: single ply with at least 30% recycled content, packaged in 500 count with recycled paper wrapping. The napkin, when folded shall measure at least six inches on each side. Rectangular napkins are acceptable, provided that the smaller side meets the minimum size.
>
> -Paper cups: 8 oz. size, with at least 10% recycled content, packaged in 50 count plastic bags. Cups must be microwave safe and shall hold either cold or warm liquids.

The example above specifies the quality and size requirements while not being restrictive. The procurement professional should always review the specifications for any restrictive requirements. A single bid might be a sign that the specifications were written such that only one company was able to meet the specified requirements. While a single bid is not always the result of a restrictive bid, it is a possible sign and should be looked into when it occurs. Taking the time to do some research can ultimately save time if there is in fact a single source. In most jurisdictions restrictive specifications have legal consequences for the agency and the procurement official. Guard your reputation and career by taking some precautionary steps against restrictive specifications. If the item or service can only be obtained from a single source, the bid process is not your "go to" process. In such case, explore the sole source process requirements of your agency.

In developing specifications for work services, make sure that you are focusing on the services and any procedures that the contractor will be expected to follow. If the contractor will be required to go through a security screening before the contractor can assess the area, make sure that it is included in the bid specifications and on the contractor onboarding process once the contract is awarded.

Example Work Service: Snow removal services

> *Contractor shall provide snow removal services for all walkway areas surrounding the City Hall building located at 1234 Main Street, Pearl City, Minnesota. Contractor shall be prepared to perform services during regular business hours and have equipment on site on the day of expected heavy snow within one (1) hour of the snowfall reaching ½ inch. Services shall be provided no later than four (4) hours after ½ inch snowfall after business hours. Contractor shall remove accumulated snow and salt area upon snow removal. Contractor must have the ability to shovel snow from areas inaccessible to snow removal equipment within the same timeframe so as to reduce risk of slip and fall accidents. Contractor must pre-salt area whenever freezing rain is announced in the weather forecast. Contractor may store equipment to be used on site in the designated area of the parking adjacent to the building.*

In the example above, the contractor may want to know the size of the space available to store the equipment and how to access it off hours or even during business hours. Specific information lowers the risk of the "unknowns" to the bidder. This reduces the risk of change orders to the agency later on.

Minimum Qualifications or Requirements

The procurement professional should make sure that the information on minimum requirements or qualifications is covered in the invitation for bid document. These are the requirements that will be used to determine if the apparent low bidder is responsible (meets the minimum qualifications to perform the work or provide the goods). Minimum qualifications or requirements shall not be restrictive so as to limit the bidders to one potentially qualified vendor. Requirements may include, among other things, financial capacity, prior relevant experience, necessary equipment, availability of qualified personnel to manage the contract or perform the work, licenses, insurance, ability to obtain bonding, certifications, and any other item that may be relevant to the scope of work or specifications. Generally, not all bidders are required to provide this information at the time of bid unless advised in the bid to do so. It is more efficient for both the organization issuing the bid and the prospective bidders to require the information from only the bidder identified as the apparent low bidder. Some organizations request the information from the three lowest bidders for expediency in the event that the apparent low bidder is deemed non-responsible.

> **Example:** *Bidder shall demonstrate relevant experience on prior projects of similar magnitude. Bidder must demonstrate that it possesses the financial capacity to undertake the work. Upon request, bidder shall provide evidence of required licenses and construction experience performing similar projects of comparable magnitude. In addition, bidder must demonstrate the financial capacity to undertake the project and experienced key personnel to successfully perform the work within the required timeframe. Prior to bid submission, bidder must file a financial statement with the CPO's office. Financial capacity will be assessed based on financial rating received from the CPO's office and the level of uncompleted work. Upon issuance of intent to accept the bid, bidder must provide evidence of insurance and bonding no later than 10 business days upon receipt of official notice of acceptance.*

Basis of Award

The basis of award establishes how the agency will be reviewing the bids. This injects transparency to the process. Some bids are stacked based on the sum of all priced items or based on a lump sum. Yet there are others that are awarded by line, group, geographical area, or even based on the sum of the base amount plus possible options being considered. There are reasons why any particular strategy works best at any given time, and the implementation of any such strategy depends on the goals of the procurement. Determining what would work best is part of the creative side of procurement where the procurement professional can add value by providing the best possible solution to the situation at hand.

When writing the basis of award, it is important to use the terminology consistently. For example, if the amount that will be considered to award the contract is labeled as "base bid or total base bid" on the price pages, use the same term in the basis of award. The consistent use of terminology will avoid confusion in the award process. The goal is to eliminate ambiguity as to how it will be determined which firm is the lowest bidder. If the basis of award is clear, you minimize the risk that the results will be challenged.

Note that the responsibility review comes after the price comparison. The goal here is to make sure that if the work was for say roofing work, the contractor has roofing experience. Responsibility is a necessary step, as it is possible that the reason why a vendor/contractor might be low is because it is inexperienced in the area and is trying to buy the project with the intent of gaining experience on your project and at the agency's expense. Generally organizations don't want to be the training ground for a new business as they are accountable to taxpayers or a board.

> **Example - Basis of Award:** *The agency will review bids for responsiveness to requirements. Bidders must provide a bid amount for each line item to be considered. All responsive bids will be stacked in ascending order of price as provided in the Total Base Bid. The City will review and make adjustments associated to arithmetic errors to ascertain whether the order of bids is correct. In the event of arithmetic errors in any of the line items, the unit price will be the controlling factor to correct the arithmetic error. The agency will not assume that an error exists in the unit price. Once this process is complete, the order of the bids will be revised as necessary. The agency will then conduct the responsibility review of the apparent lowest bidder based on the minimum qualification requirements in Section ____. If the lowest bidder is deemed responsible, then the agency will proceed with an award recommendation of the responsible bidder whose bid is responsive and the lowest based on the Total Base Bid.*

The review process can be standardized and included in the instructions to bidders section. This will allow for an abbreviated version on the basis of award section. If the evaluation process is always the same, it makes sense to standardize it. If you decide to select the abbreviated option below, please make sure that the instructions to bidders include information on the process by which the bids will be evaluated. When there are errors in the addition, it is good to be in a position to point to a process described in the bid document rather than rely on standard practice such as: "the unit price is the controlling factor and cannot be changed."

> ***Example – Abbreviated Version of Basis of Award:*** *The agency intends to award a contract to the lowest responsive and responsible bidder. Lowest price shall be determined using the Total Based Bid amount.*

Not all bids are as simple as we would like. In some instances, the end user needs options due at times to the limitation of funding; or because a single vendor cannot provide all of the goods or services or because there are other circumstances surrounding the procurement. It might be more efficient to break a large geographical area into segments when timing and cost for providing services is important. In that case, a possible outcome of the bid process is multiple awards; that is, a separate contract per segment. However, what would you do if a single vendor were the low bidder for more than one segment or all of the segments? The process followed to handle the situation depends on the circumstances and the process described in the document. The procurement professional's market research and sourcing process will help determine if the available vendors have the capacity to perform the entire scope of the work on more than one segment. This means that the research and sourcing process conducted by the procurement professional helps shape the basis of award that best meets the situation in order for the bid process to be effective. It is advantageous to spend the extra day thinking through the basis of award instead of rushing out the document and later have do rebid.

In the next example, the order in which each geographical location will be awarded is provided. This information provides transparency in the event that certain geographical areas are more desirable or financially advantageous than others. This way, contractors are less likely to claim that you are playing favorites if they don't get the most lucrative or largest geographical area.

Example – Multiple Award: The agency will review bids for responsiveness to requirements. All responsive bids will be listed in ascending order of price provided in the base bid for each geographical location, with a separate list for each geographical location. The agency will review and make adjustments associated to arithmetic errors to ascertain that the order of bids is correct. In the event of arithmetic errors in any of the line items, the unit price will be the controlling factor to correct the arithmetic error. The agency will not assume that an error exists in the unit price. Once this process is complete, the order of the bids will be revised as necessary. The agency will then conduct the responsibility review of the apparent lowest bidder based on the minimum qualification requirements in Section ____. If the lowest bidder is deemed responsible, then the agency will proceed with an award recommendation of the responsible bidder whose bid is responsive and the lowest based on the total base bid for that segment. If a bidder is the apparent low bidder in more than one geographical area, its capacity to perform the work in more than one area will be evaluated. For purposes of evaluation, the agency will consider capacity for award based on the following order: Segment A-North; Segment B-Central; Segment C-South; Segment D-East; Segment E-West

Price

Price is a determining factor provided that the bid is responsive and the bidder is ultimately responsible to perform the work or provide the goods. Sometimes agencies use the terms cost and price interchangeably. Cost refers to the components of the total price. It's just a technicality, but you are looking for the fully loaded amount of what the organization will need to pay for the item(s) rather than having to perform the calculation every time you purchase an item. The cost components might be relevant in other types of procurement, but generally not in bids. The bid document should require bidders to complete a specific form. The form can be electronic. The uniform submission of price will facilitate price comparison and analysis. The standardization will save time in the process.

BID EVALUATION

The objective of the bid, as stated before, is to select the vendor that submits the lowest price and meets the minimum qualifications to perform the services or provide the goods. Bids are reviewed and listed in ascending order by price, identifying the lowest at each step of the bid review and evaluation process.

The basis of award will determine the order of the bids, which is why the basis of award must be very clear in the IFB document. The identification of the apparent low bidder at the public bid opening is a preliminary result. The procurement professional must perform a review of the bids submitted to make sure that they pass the responsiveness test. Bids are either responsive or they are not. There are no varying degrees of responsiveness. Responsive bids are stacked to identify the apparent low bidder. It remains "apparent" until the responsibility review is completed. The responsibility review is an important step that is often missed by less experienced procurement professionals. The apparent low bidder must meet the minimum qualifications and/or requirements in order to actually be considered the low bidder. Once the responsibility review is complete and the apparent low bidder is determined to be responsible, then it becomes the low bidder. The lowest responsive and responsible bidder is moved to the recommendation and/or award process in accordance with the organization's established procedures.

SUMMARY

The bid process can be a very efficient way to enter into contracts for goods and routine general work or services needed within your organization if used correctly. There are some variations of the bid process developed over the years to respond to specific needs. Some agencies have adopted such variations of the bid process, but knowing the basics will help make a determination if the variation is appropriate at the time of bid document development. It is important to carefully align the method and process with the type of goods and services to more effectively utilize the organization's resources. The right method can save time and improve agency efficiencies.

CHAPTER II
Request for Qualifications (RFQ)

Certain types of services may require a qualifications-based selection. This is generally the case for architectural and engineering services in the public sector. The RFQ is a competitive procurement method, but should not be the first choice unless there it is necessary to achieve the goals of the project. Procurement professionals should consult the legal requirements applicable to the organization.

At times, this process is used as a first step in a longer process for complex projects or certain programs. The RFQ process is advantageous on highly complex, multi- discipline procurements. It allows the organization to further explore business opportunities only with those firms or teams deemed qualified. That is, the respondents that demonstrated to be the highest qualified according to the evaluation criteria. The RFQ process affords the organization the opportunity to focus only on those vendors that will ultimately be considered. This avoids a very expensive investment of time and resources for both the organization issuing the RFQ and the businesses interested getting the contract for the specific project. It should be noted that using the RFQ when another method is more appropriate will elongate the procurement process and may cause frustration of those involved.

The terminology used in an RFQ is different from a bid. In an RFQ process, the response submitted is generally referred to a "submittal" or "qualifications." The vendor submitting the response is referred to as the "respondent."

OBJECTIVE AND APPLICATION

Objective
The objective of a qualification-based selection is to identify the highest qualified firm(s) for the specific purpose or scope of services.

Application
This method is generally appropriate when it is required by law, when it is part of a two-step or multi-step process, or to establish a list of pre-qualified firms for a specific purpose from which price proposals or bids will be requested at a later date. It requires a more in-depth responsibility review than the bid process. In the case of a pre-qualified list, no additional responsibility review is performed unless specifically stated in the prequalification program or for a specific project.

RFQ DEVELOPMENT
When developing an RFQ, think of three areas: The Overview (Big Picture); The Project or Program; and The Evaluation and Selection Requirements. It is easy to standardize the format and certain portions of the RFQ, such as: the background of the organization, the evaluation process, the organization-specific forms, and any other directives that may be required in every procurement process conducted by the organization. Developing a format with these standard sections may save some time in the development of the document. It is advisable to always start with a fresh format and not modify the last RFQ issued. The opportunity for errors is high when a previously issued RFQ is used as the starting document for a new RFQ.

Overview
The overview is simply a high level view of the project and the environment or situation under which services will be provided.

1. Purpose Statement: Provide a sentence or two to briefly describe the reason for the RFQ.

Example 1: The City of Mountainside seeks qualifications from interested firms to provide structural design engineering services for the design and construction of the bridge over the Dustin River.

> **Example 2:** The State of Sunshine is seeking qualifications for structural engineering consulting for the design of various State-maintained bridges throughout the State. The State intends to establish a list of pre-qualified firms to perform the services for one or more of the bridges.

2. Background about the Organization: Provide a description of the organization, its purpose, and what it represents. You may find a paragraph or two on the agency's website. The description helps provide context to the project, it's similar to describing the setting of a story.

> **Example 1:** The City of Mountainside is in a valley surrounded by the Smokey Mountains and is a tourist destination for campers and hikers. The City has doubled its population over the last 10 years ...

> **Example 2:** The State of Sunshine is one of the largest states in the nation serving a population of four million residents in nearly 100 municipalities, villages, and townships...

> 3. Problem Statement and/or Goals: Indicate what the organization wants to achieve. If there is a problem to be solved, describe the problem, indicate the intended outcome or goals sought to be achieved by contracting with the successful respondent. The examples below provide a description of the situation and states the goals of the agency.

> **Example 1:** The City has received funding to replace the aging bridge over the Dustin River. In replacing the bridge, the City wants to address the added demand due to the population growth and provide a design that can address future growth and traffic requirements on the bridge route.

> The City is seeking a professional structural engineering consultant to provide an assessment with recommendations to the City officials and develop a design in accordance with the results of the assessment and consultation with the City officials....

Example 2: *The State has secured funding for the recon-struction and refurbishing of state bridges. The projects will be implemented over the next five years. Some of the bridges will need to be completely demolished and replaced while maintaining temporary access to commut-ers. Others will require alternate access for commuters. The State selected an architectural design firm under a design competition process. The design firm created a conceptual design for the bridges. The conceptual design reflects the brand of a progressive state and well planned structures.*

It is the State's desire to achieve a consistent look that iden-tifies the bridge with the State. The consistency in design throughout the state will also provide ease of maintenance and achieve economies of scale in the purchase of sup-plies for the maintenance of bridges...

THE PROJECT OR PROGRAM

Unlike the bid, the level of detail provided in this section for the RFQ is not pre-scriptive. Instead, it provides a set of guidelines or expectations of the firm that will ultimately perform the services or participate in the program.

1. Scope of Services: The scope of services builds on the goals established in the problem/goals above. It specifies the services being sought without being prescriptive. The scope of services may include a list of tasks or responsibilities that the respondent will be required to perform if awarded the contract. Similar to the job description in a hiring situation, the more comprehensive or clear the list of tasks or responsibilities are, the easier it will be to evaluate the qualifica-tions and experience of respondents in order to determine the best qualified respondent for the project. Vague descriptions may have undesirable results. Unlike the bid method, the RFQ does not offer details on how the services will be provided. It is seeking someone or a firm that is qualified to develop a solution or implement a project.

Example: *The selected respondent(s) will be required to incorporate the architectural design into the final engi-neering design. The structural design engineering team will be required to make the necessary design adjustments based on the site and develop detailed drawings and specifications for construction. The selected respondent(s) will also be required to provide oversight during construction including resident engineering services ....*

2. Other Requirements: Qualifications-based procurements are heavily based on the credentials of the firms and personnel proposed to perform the services. The fact that you select this method says that you have already made that determination. It is, therefore, important that it be made clear that the respondents do not have flexibility to replace the firm(s), if a team, or the key personnel who have been offered to perform the services. If the selection were to be based on a firm's qualifications or the qualifications of its key personnel, it wouldn't make sense to allow the replacement of the firms or personnel after the contract is awarded. This would change the profile of the respondent, unless the replacement results in equal or better qualifications. I recommend that you add a requirement regarding substitution of key personnel. For example, since the criterion for key personnel might be heavily weighted in a qualifications based process, then you may want to include a condition that prohibits the substitution of key personnel without proper express approval from an authorized representative of the agency.

> **Example** - *Key Personnel: The Respondent shall identify key personnel for the project. Key personnel is a key component of the criteria by which the Respondent will be selected; therefore, Respondent will not have the ability to replace key personnel until they complete the tasks assigned based on the role proposed, unless there are extenuating circumstances. Any substitutions shall require prior written approval by an authorized representative of the City (agency), and the City (agency) will accept only personnel whose credentials are equal or better than the key personnel for which substitution is sought.*

This section of the RFQ should include any other requirements deemed important for the project's success. I don't recommend including all of the contract terms in this section. It is more efficient to include the contract terms as an attachment. In this section, include only those special provisions that you want to highlight and that are relevant to the success of the project. I advise to use simple business language instead of elaborate legal language when highlighting the additional requirements. The objective is clarity.

When the purpose of the RFQ is to establish a list of pre-qualified firms, I caution you not to make the purpose generic. Once you've established that a firm or team is qualified under the generic terms, you may find yourself locked inside a box with a firm that has no relevant experience for a particular project and yet the firm has been pre-qualified.

Case Study: A government agency responsible for major design and construction of public buildings decided to establish pre-qualified lists of contractors for trade work and general construction. The agency wanted to issue the RFQ quickly and did not take the time to identify types of projects. Since the scope for pre-qualification under the general construction category was so generic, the result of the exercise was a list of general contractors with a very wide range of qualifications and experience. Once the bids for construction started to go out, there were contractors whose largest project did not reach $1,000,000. Since they had been pre-qualified to do general construction work for the agency, they were bidding on $15MM projects. The pre-qualification process established that these firms were qualified; therefore, it made it very difficult to limit the pool of contractors to those that had comparable project experience. By conducting the pre-qualification process without establishing categories of work or parameters, the agency had essentially conducted the responsibility step, which deemed all pre-qualified to be responsible. The agency had no justification to deny the award of a contract to a firm that had not performed a project of that magnitude. Fortunately for both the agency and the firm, the contractor was unable to obtain the necessary bonding to perform the work, and the agency was able to award the contract to the next lowest bidder who had the experience and capacity to perform the work.

> The agency later hired a Procurement Director and the first order of business was to fix the prequalification process. The new prequalification process included descriptions of the types of projects that the agency normally performed and prequalified the contractors based on those types of projects. It also included a secondary review of capacity to take place at the time of award. This prevented a contractor from being awarded multiple contracts simultaneously without having the capacity to undertake all of them successfully. Since this was a condition of prequalification, the agency was on better ground to make decisions in the best interest of the agency and taxpayers.

Example – Additional Due Diligence: *Pre-qualified contrac-tors will be eligible to participate on bids under which the contractor has been deemed qualified. The City will review the capacity and past performance of the contractor prior to the award of a contract. The City may elect not to award a contract to the apparent low bidder if the City determines that the bidder does not have the capacity to undertake the project at the time of award or has unre-solved performance issues in prior awards. The decision will be based on the City's best interest.*

In the example above the agency included a provision in their prequalification program that allows further evaluation on a project-by-project basis. This pro-vision in the RFQ document alerts prospective contractors that additional due diligence will be conducted by the agency prior to contract award.

PROCESS AND REQUIREMENTS FOR EVALUATION AND SELECTION

Evaluation and Selection Process: The process should be transparent but have a certain level of flexibility at the same time. Using words like "may" will provide options to skip steps such as presentations, if it is determined that they are not necessary.

Example: *The CPO or authorized representative will review submittals received and determine responsiveness. A com-mittee led by Procurement and comprised by represen-tatives of various departments will evaluate responsive submittals in accordance with the evaluation criteria listed in this RFQ. The preliminary result of that evaluation may cause the committee to shortlist the respondents that best meet the criteria. Shortlisted respondents may be invited to submit clarifications and/or make presentation(s) following specific City (agency) requirements. The City reserves the right to solicit reference information from other parties not specifically identified in the respondent's submittal.*

Upon completion of the evaluation, the evaluation commit-tee will rank respondents based on the results of the evalua-tions and identify the respondents who have demonstrated to be the best qualified to perform the services. The rec-ommendation will be presented to the Department Head for selection approval. The final selection will be submitted to the CPO for concurrence. Upon concurrence with the selection, contract negotiations will be initiated with the selected firm. If negotiations are not successful, the City (agency) may terminate negotiations and begin contract negotiations with the next highest ranked respondent.

The final selection and negotiated contract will be submitted to the governing body, as appropriate, for final approval and execution.

If the agency is seeking to establish a list of pre-qualified firms, then the agency may or may not negotiate contracts. Instead the agency may choose to notify the successful respondents and may seek project-specific proposals when the opportunity arises. It is important to customize the process to fit the purpose.

Example: *The CPO or authorized representative will review submittals received and determine responsiveness. A committee led by Procurement and comprised by representatives of various departments will evaluate responsive submittals received in accordance with the evaluation criteria specified for this RFQ. The preliminary result may cause the committee to shortlist the respondents that best meet the criteria. Shortlisted respondents may be invited to submit clarifications and/or make presentation(s) following specific City (agency) requirements. The City (agency) may solicit reference information from other agencies or organizations not specifically listed in the respondent's submittal. The evaluation committee will rank the shortlisted respondent based on the final evaluation.*

The prequalified list of respondents will be presented to the Department Head for approval. The approved pre-qualified list of respondents will be submitted to the CPO for concurrence. The CPO will establish the list of prequalified firms and solicit proposals as need arises.

Or - The City may enter into master agreements and issue task orders under such agreements as projects are identified.

<u>Evaluation Criteria</u>: Once submittals are received, the evaluation can be divided into two steps: responsiveness and qualification requirements. This will facilitate the evaluation process later on. I generally like to order the criteria in descending order of importance. It is helpful to be able to segregate what is truly important for the specific scope and what is a more general business practice or agency requirement. The example below shows the first criterion and the first step in the evaluation process.

> **Example:** *The submittals will be evaluated and accordance with the following criteria in each of the areas below. Respondents must be successful in the first area in order to progress to the next. That is, only those responsive submittals will be evaluated and ranked.*
>
> 1. **Responsiveness:** *Does the submittal substantially conform to RFQ submission requirements necessary to evaluate the submittal?*

Similar to the RFP, the first step in the evaluation process is to determine if the submittals meet all of the requirements necessary for the evaluation team to actually conduct the evaluation in accordance with the criteria. The submission of the information required will allow the evaluation committee to make a recommendation, based on the criteria, of qualified firms that should be shortlisted and/or placed on the prequalification list, as appropriate. That is, any relevant information necessary to make that determination must have been submitted. If the evaluation committee is not able to evaluate the submittal on a criterion or multiple criteria, then the submittal should not be considered responsive to all the material portions of the RFQ. This is not to be confused with the absence of a routine check mark on a form or an error that can be corrected administratively; unless of course that check mark is crucial or the error significantly alters the quality of the submittal.

Note that the responsiveness step is a pass or fail result. The submittal is either responsive or it is not.

The second step in the process is to evaluate all responsive submittals. The purpose here is to determine how well and to what extent the respondents' qualifications align with the criteria. It is important to draft the criteria in a way that it is relevant to the scope of the RFQ. The procurement professional must make sure that the criteria will help make a good assessment of the qualifications and that the criteria are relevant to the scope of the project.

Notice that the price is not a consideration in RFQs. The qualifications are the determining factor. In the case of a single selection, the committee will generally establish a ranking hierarchy based on the qualifications. The goal with an RFQ is to select the best qualified. If, on the other hand, the goal is to establish a list of pre-qualified firms, those firms ranking the highest should make the list.

In the example below, the first two or three of the criteria are the most relevant to the outcome of the RFQ process and the primary purpose of the RFQ, which is to identify the highest qualified respondent(s). In the case of a pre-qualification process, the first two may carry the most weight in the evaluation process. Generally, a respondent whose credentials to perform the services are unclear or questionable should not make the shortlist in the evaluation process. When a respondent of questionable or unclear qualifications ends up in the shortlist, it may be the result of a defective evaluation process or rating structure.

Example-cont.:
Technical or Qualification Requirements: All responsive submittals will be evaluated based on the criteria listed below. The criteria are listed in descending order of importance.

a. *Professional qualifications and experience of the team as evidenced by relevant projects of similar scope and complexity.*

b. *Professional qualifications and (specialized) experience of key personnel to successfully perform the services as evidenced by their prior experience in similar roles in comparable projects.*

c. *Understanding of the goals and approach to successfully perform the services as evidenced by the quality of the plan of action and its relevance to the project described in this RFQ.*

d. *Capacity of the key personnel and the ability to commit adequate time to effectively perform the services in the role assigned.*

e. Local availability of key personnel to facilitate implementation.

f. Financial stability of the respondent and its capacity to effectively undertake the project.

g. Ability to meet (list all other agency) requirements.

The level of importance of the criteria will depend on the project's nature and the goals of the organization. When establishing the criteria and the relative weight of each criterion to be used in the evaluation process, it's important to keep in mind not to let less relevant or less important criteria outweigh criteria that would directly impact the success of the project. I will expand on this point when I talk about the evaluation process.

3. Submittal Requirements: This section lets the prospective respondents know how to submit, what to submit, how many copies, and where to submit their response to the RFQ. If there are specific format requirements, they should be described clearly.

Format: Some organizations have this portion standardized and language is included in all procurements. It is a good idea to review it anyway and make any updates or adjustments as necessary.

> **Example** - Format: Please submit one original and ____ copies of response printed on recycled paper 8-½" X 11", single-sided, and bound on the left side. Information shall be organized in the order listed below separated by labeled tabs. Electronic copies shall be submitted in CD ROM (or USB) format. (Indicate the number of soft copy material.) Expensive paper and binding are discouraged as the agency will not return submittals nor will it compensate the respondent for any expenses associated with respondent's participation in this process.

When specifying the format, don't ask respondents to submit in a way that conforms to the latest trend; instead, opt for the format that your organization is ready to support. Some agencies request electronic copies but fall short on the technology to support the electronic review. This will result in the procurement professional having to make copies for each of the evaluation team members, in addition to binding and distributing them. Depending on the size and number of submittals, you've added at least two to three days to the process, not to mention the work that may be falling behind because of the additional work that you created for yourself and the frustration of evaluation team members who were unable to view the submittals electronically. While I would choose the environmentally friendly option every time I can, it is important to also be practical.

Content: The content of the RFQ response depends largely on the evaluation criteria. Remember, the submittal requirements provide the information that the evaluation team needs to evaluate the respondent under each criterion. The information required also helps the procurement professional determine if a valid submission has been made, and if the respondent has met the other requirements of the organization. The submittal requirements must be in sync with the evaluation criteria. Syncing the submittal requirements to the evaluation criteria will help the evaluation committee to systematically review and evaluate the submittals.

Important Note: For purposes of illustration, the submittal requirements below are synced with the evaluation criteria in the example above. The actual submittal requirements will vary depending on the project scope. The logic of including each submittal requirement listed is provided for your benefit.

Example:
Content: *In order to evaluate submittals uniformly, please provide the documents and information listed below.*

1) **Cover Letter.** *The cover letter shall indicate the names of the firms comprising the team, the name and contact information of each lead person, and a statement committing to provide the services as proposed with the key personnel identified. The letter should also state that its author is an authorized representative of the team.*

2) **Executive Summary:** *The executive summary shall be brief and include the Respondent's understanding of the goals and a summary of the proposed strategy. Describe why and how the team is qualified to perform the services by providing a brief summary of the experience of the firms (prime and subcontractors). If team members have worked* *together in other projects, please provide the name of the project.*

The cover letter will provide information that will allow the procurement professional to establish a list of respondents, team members, and contacts. Being able to develop a matrix or a list of respondents with information about the members of the team will be a useful tool throughout the procurement process. The cover letter will satisfy the requirement of having the response submitted by "an authorized representative of the respondent." This will allow the team to establish the validity of the submittal. Some agencies have a specific form for execution. If the response is valid, the respondent can be bound to the representations made on the submittal if the respondent were to be selected to perform the services.

It is generally a good idea to request an executive summary. An executive summary is extremely helpful on large projects. Well-written executive summaries can give you the high level information that the procurement professional or the evaluation team members may need throughout the process.

Since the next two to three submittal requirements correspond to the most important criteria, I recommend being very specific and clear about the information to be submitted. It helps to develop a form that captures only the experience information that you need to make a determination. Free form responses may include an abundance of information that may not be needed and may require evaluation team members to sift through it to find the information that is actually needed; or, on the other hand, the response may not provide enough information to make a determination.

> *3)* **Qualifications of the Firms:** *Provide a list of relevant projects performed in the last five (5) years. Include the name of the project, a brief description, the dollar value, date of performance, and contact information (name, title, organization, phone number and email address). Also, include the names of key personnel in this RFQ that participated in the project. If respondent is comprised of a team of firms, respondent shall provide this information for each of the firms.*
>
> *4)* **Qualifications of Key Personnel.** *Submit chronological resumes for each key personnel. Provide a list of projects in*

which key personnel performed in a similar role to that proposed. Reference information shall include a brief description of the project, the dollar value, the role performed, and contact information (name, title, phone number, and email address). Also, indicate if the key personnel performed any work in the projects referenced for the firm(s) above.

5) **Understanding** and **Approach.** Provide a project plan for the performance of the services and project implementation, including but not limited to the description of the methodology for implementation and project management.

Attach a proposed schedule depicting key milestones and any critical path items, as appropriate. (A schedule may not be appropriate in the case of a prequalification.)

Include an organization chart depicting the name, role of each key personnel, and the firm. If there are subcontractors or firms partnering, indicate the role of each firm.

6) **Teams Capacity:** Provide a chart of key personnel and their availability for the project particularly during the time of their proposed involvement in the project. Provide information and level of commitment to other projects and the expected date of completion of those commitments.

7) **Local Availability of Key Personnel:** Provide a list of key personnel that will be locally available during their performance on the project. Also, include information on planned relocations or if key personnel will be traveling frequently on project matters.

8) **Financial Stability:** Provide financial statements for the last three fiscal years. At a minimum, the information provided shall include the opinion letter, balance sheet, auditor's notes, and any schedules to support balance sheet.

9) **Other Requirements:** Add other agency or project-specific requirements or organization's standard forms, as appropriate

Providing a form or a format for submission is generally helpful to focus on only that information necessary at the time of evaluation, particularly if the number of submittals received or the volume of the submittals expected may seem overwhelming to the evaluation committee members. Spending the necessary time to flush this section out is an investment towards efficiency to be realized at the evaluation stage.

h. <u>Place and Deadline for Submission</u>: There is no room for error in this section; therefore, please double and triple check to make sure that you are providing the correct information. Dates often change from the first draft; therefore, please make sure the dates are correct. Ask a coworker to review it for you. Many agencies provide this information on the cover page of the RFQ for emphasis. That's ideal; however, it also makes sense to keep all submission instructions in a single section as more details can be provided. If you decide to duplicate the information, it is crucial that no discrepancies occur. At a minimum, the submission instructions should include the following: date and time of submission, address where submittals will be received, RFQ identification (number, title), contact person for the procurement, information on how late submittals will be handled particularly if a third party is hired to deliver submittals, and information on how to submit questions or register to receive any addenda or clarifications issued by the agency.

Example:
Responses shall be submitted no later than _____ on _____. Late proposals will/shall (depends on your agency's policy) not be accepted after the date and time of the specified herein.

Submittal shall be delivered to:

Procurement Number

Name of Agency

Submitted to the attention of:

Physical address where the Proposal shall be delivered

Pre-Submittal Conference: (date, time, location)

Deadline for the submission of questions:

Submit any questions in writing to: _____ via email no later than the deadline for questions indicated above.

The (agency) may issue addenda or clarifications prior to the due date and time for the RFQ submission. In order to receive notifications, each prospective respondent must register on the (agency's) website. Prospective respondents must download the RFQ after registering in order to be notified or receive any addenda or clarifications issued for this RFQ.

If delivery of the submittal is made by courier service, submittals must be received at the correct location no later than the time and date specified. It is the responsibility of the Respondent to see that the delivery is made as required in this RFQ.

Exhibits and Forms

Simplifying the document may require that some of the information be attached as exhibits or attachments. Include these once you have dealt with the process, criteria, and submission requirements. This section contains all of the standard forms, boilerplate, and exhibits. Place any exhibits related to the RFQ scope and submission first, then any boilerplate or forms that all vendors are expected to complete or execute. It is a good idea to include a draft of the contract that the selected respondent will be expected to sign. Any exceptions taken to the standard contract can be reviewed internally ahead of time. Doing so generally shortens the contract negotiations later. Some agencies include a criterion regarding exceptions taken by respondents to the standard contracts. The purpose of doing that is to consider the exceptions as part of the evaluation process and thus determine whether or not a contract with the respondent is feasible or if there will be major hurdles to overcome in the negotiations. Exceptions can extend the length of negotiations, which in turn can impact the cost of doing business for both the respondent and the organization.

RFQ EVALUATION PROCESS

As stated before, the objective of the RFQ is to identify the best-qualified firm(s) for selection or to establish a list of pre-qualified firms to later request price or a more detailed submission for a specific project.

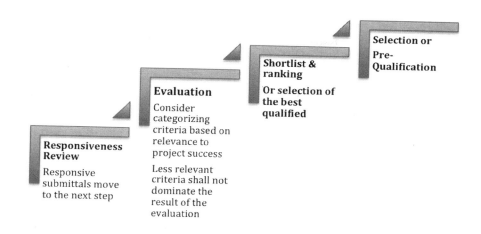

Responsiveness Review

Responsive submittals move to the next step

Evaluation

Consider categorizing criteria based on relevance to project success

Less relevant criteria shall not dominate the result of the evaluation

Shortlist & ranking

Or selection of the best qualified

Selection or Pre-Qualification

All submissions go through the responsiveness review. Only those responsive submittals move on to the second step, which it is the evaluation of qualifications. This is the heart of the evaluation process. The result of this step may represent a business opportunity for those selected to be on the shortlist or prequalification list or even be awarded a contract. As I mentioned before, how each criterion is weighted matters and will impact the final result of the process. There are criteria that are considered critical to the success of the project and to which more emphasis is given in the review of submittals. A second type of criteria might be considered important overall, but certain ambiguities can be corrected through clarifications or as the full scope of the project and circumstances are revealed. The third type of criteria is that where compliance is required and minor errors may be corrected administratively through further conversations.

This third type of criteria refers to process requirements such as the submission of certain forms. While the submission may be required and considered in the responsiveness review, the agency may need additional information from the vendor before a contract is awarded. An example of this is an ownership disclosure statement form. The vendor may have submitted the form and provided the ownership disclosure statement that it believed was required. Upon a more detailed review it is determined that additional information is needed to fully understand the ownership structure of the company. The submission of that additional ownership information does not change whether they will be able to perform the services, but understanding the ownership structure may be necessary to determine the entity that will actually be liable for any failure to perform.

Perhaps the clarification is needed to determine what financial assurances the agency will have to recover any loss associated with a performance failure. The ownership may be more relevant in some projects than others. If ownership is critical to the success of the project, then the criterion should have a different weight and not categorized under this third category. Seasoned procurement professionals may have come across that one form where they put a great deal of effort generally because it is hard to understand. The logical thing to do would be to change it, but that may be easier said than done. Changing it may require an extensive process and the engagement of a good number of people in the organization. While that process takes place, procurement professionals need the flexibility to work with what they have or reject every proposal that fails to submit the information perfectly. It seems only fair not to penalize vendors and staff because of organizational sensitivities around a form.

When developing the evaluation instructions and scoring or rating strategy, it's important to keep the weight given to each criterion in mind. If the same weight is applied and the process calls for simply adding the results for each criterion or even averaging the scores of all evaluators, the result may not be what is desired as it may not reflect the quality of the submittals accurately. It is therefore that I make the recommendations below:

1. **Separate Criteria:** Categorize the criteria by determining the individual value and relevancy to the success of the project.

2. **Give Purpose To Criteria:** If a criterion is critical to the success of the project, do not shortlist submittals that do not at least receive an acceptable rating or score in that criterion.

3. **Define Scoring Qualitatively:** If you elect to use numeric scoring, define what it means to receive a specific score. This will allow you to translate a score into a qualitative explanation and differentiate the relevance of the scores particularly when the difference comes down to one or two points.

4. **Address Impact of Substandard Scores:** Determine ahead of time how you will handle poor or unacceptable scores in any of the criteria. If a criterion made it to the list of criteria, it must have had some level of importance; and it doesn't make sense to accept a poor score or rating.

5. **Strengths and Weaknesses:** Require evaluation team members to justify the rating or score by focusing on strengths and weaknesses. This will help reduce subjectivity in the process. The comments that the evaluation team members provide will help make the recommendation and award process go more smoothly. Summarize the evaluation process and use comments to highlight the reasons why the ranking, and ultimately the recommendation, is credible. Also, no additional work will be required to conduct debriefings later on. It's much easier to collect these comments as the evaluation progresses rather than to have to go back to evaluation team members and request their reasons once the evaluation process is complete.

6. I have tested an evaluation method using the recommendations above for at least 20 years with different types of procurements, particularly those surrounded by controversy. Even when the results were challenged in court, the process served to further confirm that it produced a solid result. It may seem simpler to throw some scores and add them up; but, in the end, having to go back and justify the scores may be more time consuming than asking everyone in the evaluation committee to contribute to the rationale for selection while the information is fresh in their heads.

SUMMARY

When drafting an RFQ, first make an effort to understand what the end user is seeking making sure that requirements are clearly articulated in the RFQ document. Organize the document in a logical manner so that information is easy to follow. Keep the end in mind. Always ask yourself and the end user what will a successful process produce and what do you need to achieve the results desired from a qualitative perspective. Remember that the way in which you approach the development of the RFQ will set you apart or bury you in the crowd of bureaucrats pushing paper day in and day out. Stay away from the robotic process of feeding information into a standard document without adding value to the process. There are plenty of routine tasks that are mechanical in nature. This is not one. It is the procurement professional's critical thinking that adds value to the process.

CHAPTER III
Request For Proposals (RFP)

The RFP process is more complex than a bid or the RFQ and requires thoughtful attention to the goals that the agency desire to achieve in hiring a consultant/contractor who will, upon selection, assist the organization by providing the solution or services that the organization is seeking. Since it is a more complex process, it should not be your first choice unless it is determined that it is the method that is most suitable to select the firm that can successfully assist the organization achieve its goals.

As far as terminology in the RFP process, the responses submitted are referred to as "proposals" and the firms submitting the response are referred to as "proposers."

OBJECTIVE AND APPLICATION

Objective

The goal of the RFP is to achieve the best value, a balance between quality and price -- two competing interests. The outcome of the process may not always be the best-qualified proposer or the best price, but the proposer that demonstrates high quality at a price acceptable to the organization. There are some occasions when the highest-qualified proposer also offers an affordable or competitive price. This is, of course, the best possible scenario. I caution you not to use this process to provide "flexibility" in the selection process. That statement may be misinterpreted as a process that is not truly transparent and one that may be contested by proposers as being ambiguous. The RFP is a competitive procurement method and vendors are expecting a transparent process where they are offered a fair opportunity to compete for your agency's business.

Application

This process is generally appropriate when procuring certain professional or consulting services, if price consideration is not legally prohibited; the project is complex and includes a combination of professional services, computer equipment and software; the agency is seeking to solve a particular problem; or when the agency seeks value-added services to an otherwise routine service, which cannot be specifically identified in the procurement document.

If the end users are strongly urging you to do an RFP because they are not clear on what they desire and just want to check the market, it might be best to start with an Request for Information (RFI). This research tool will afford the end user the opportunity to understand what the market has to offer; will help the end user articulate the goals and scope of the project; and avoid unnecessary cost and effort of those involved. The RFP process is too costly and requires too large of an investment of time and resources for both the agency and the vendors to use as a research tool. The RFI is a worthwhile investment that can to make the RFP process more effective.

RFP DEVELOPMENT

If your organization has a standard format and boilerplate language for the RFP, you may need to do more than simply insert the scope and publish the document. The document needs to be customized for the specific project so that its components fit logically and the evaluation committee can make a fair assessment of the proposals in relation to the project. Once you understand the logic that goes into preparing the RFP document, the standard documents will save you some time without converting the RFP development into a "spec sandwich" assembly exercise *(credits to my friend Michael for the term)*.

A good RFP follows a logical flow. We've already established that the purpose of issuing the RFP is to assist the organization select the vendor that will help said organization achieve the goals that caused the need for the RFP in the first place. A set of boilerplate criteria or submittal requirements may not be a one-size fits all solution. The goals of the RFP drive the development of the scope of services. The criteria and submittal requirements will later help the evaluation committee recommend the proposer offering the best value in relation to the scope of services in order to meet the goals of the project. It is, therefore, important that the criteria and submittal requirements be in alignment with the scope and goals of the project. It is the procurement professional's responsibility to see that the document achieves that alignment. Otherwise, the evaluation committee will have a difficult time reconciling information to the criteria and the overall goals of the project. The RFP should also clearly articulate the procurement requirements and facilitate a process of selecting a firm/team that demonstrates the best chance of achieving the goals of the project.

The RFP is comparable to the human resources hiring process. There is a purpose, the role, qualifications requirements, and possibly preferred credentials. The organization is generally prepared to pay the budgeted amount for the candidate that appears to be the best fit or that best meets the qualification requirements. There are times when the candidate deemed best qualified is unaffordable to the organization based on the budget. It is possible that either the requirements were not aligned with the pay scale or what the candidate has to offer is more than what the position requires. In that case, the organization makes a decision on whether the budget for the position is too low or if the organization can meet its goals with the qualified candidate that is also affordable to the organization or at the amount budgeted.

For ease of RFP development, we'll divide the components into three areas: 1) The Overview or Big Picture; 2) The Project (scope of services and requirements); and 3) The Evaluation Process and Requirements for Selection.

Overview
This first section provides an overview and puts the service and project in context.

1. <u>Purpose Statement</u>: Provide a sentence or two indicating the purpose of the procurement. The title of the procurement generally has enough information to construct a sentence or two that state the purpose succinctly.

Example: The City of Seaport seeks proposals from qualified firms to provide consulting services for the implementation of a city-wide permit system to assist the City achieve a centralized source of information for all types of permits issued by the City.

If we assume that the title of the RFP is "RFP for the Implementation of a Citywide Permit System," then developing the one of two sentences should not be difficult.

2. <u>Background of the Organization</u>: Similar to the RFQ, describe the organization, its purpose, and what it represents. This information may already be on the agency's website. A short paragraph or two should suffice. This part is optional, but putting context to the project is beneficial and, in some instances, helps proposers assess the magnitude or complexity of project implementation.

Example 1: The City of Seaport is a coastal city along the southern east shores of the United States. It is home to many historical homes and buildings that date back to the early 1800s. The total population is approximately 150,000 including the annexed areas. The residents are proud of the historic value of the City and have an active historic preservation council formed by residents and businesses passionate about the historic value of its structures.

Example 2: The Southern State University is a world-class research organization located in the City of Destination and serving 14,000 students. With a faculty of 500 and over $50MM in grants annually, the University is a premier higher education institution providing high quality education and contributing knowledge through its research. In the last five years, the University has seen rapid growth and increased interest from students around the world....

3. <u>Problem Statement and/or Goals</u>: Indicate what the agency wants to achieve. If there is a problem to be solved, describe the problem and indicate the intended outcome or goals sought to achieve by contracting with the successful proposer. Notice that in the example below the goals of the agency associated with the procurement are clearly stated.

Example 1: The City of Seashore currently has various systems to assist personnel in the permitting process. These systems are not connected and often require double entry of information before such information can be useful for any analysis. The duplicative tasks are very time-consuming requiring staff to devote an inordinate amount of time daily to data entry. With the increase in volume over the last several years, the City will need to significantly increase staffing levels to effectively keep up with the data entry tasks in order to perform needed analyses.

Instead, the City is seeking to implement a system to minimize the data entry effort by eliminating duplicative efforts; facilitate the collection of data in the office and the field; automate routine reports; and provide the capabilities for ad hoc analyses and reports.

Example 2: In the last year, the University outlined new strategic goals to maintain and/or enhance the quality of the education while addressing the growth of student population, improve efficiency of the administrative services, and expand efforts to increase research funding; however, it has not developed a detailed plan to put the strategic goals into action.

The University desires to develop a comprehensive strategic plan in alignment with the strategic goals; the plan shall provide for staff engagement at different levels; it shall identify key milestones so as to make the achievement of goals more feasible; and it shall establish performance metrics in order to measure progress towards the achievement of such strategic goals.

The Project

The project section provides information related to requirements and any details associated with the services that the successful proposer is be required to perform. Clarity surrounding performance expectations and areas that the successful proposer must address is a very important element, as the vendors interested will be putting together a proposal to respond to the requirements and providing pricing for those services. Lack of clarity may result in a very long process or a repeat process. If the performance expectations are unclear, there is a greater potential for questions and needed clarifications throughout the RFP process.

1. <u>Scope of Services</u>: The end user should be able to provide the necessary information to insert in this section. The procurement professional can help the end user flush this out by asking questions, such as: What are the expectations once the successful proposer is identified? What tasks does the end user expect the successful proposer to perform once selected and under contract? Are there any requirements that the proposer will need to abide by in order to perform the services? Are there any specific restrictions? What is the expected role of the selected proposer? What will the successful proposer be expected to provide? Will they need to be on site or can personnel work remotely? The procurement professional can assist the end user to clearly articulate the scope of services. This may require a brainstorming exercise and possibly transporting yourself and the end user to an imaginary scenario in the future when the successful proposer is identified. For example, imagine that the proposer is already on board, what does the end user expect the proposer to do? What will the ideal proposer do to make the project a success? Perhaps starting with a list of tasks or responsibilities can help flush out ideas for the development of the scope of services. Continue the exercise by defining the type of consultant and qualifications needed to perform successfully.

The scope of services is comparable to the job description when hiring an employee. The job description or scope is written with the goals in mind. The scope of services is directly related to the tasks that will need to be performed to achieve the goals of the project. Unlike the scope of work or specifications in an IFB, the scope of services in the RFP is not prescriptive. It does not provide the detail on the methods to perform the services or the specific procedures that it must follow. There are some expectations and responsibilities, but the process or method to achieve the goals is the responsibility of the proposer. How they plan to perform the services or implement the project should be part of their plan of action in their proposal. The example below is written in the context of Example 1 above to help demonstrate the connection to the high level information offered in the overview.

Example: The selected proposer will be required to:

---

1. Provide an assessment of the needs. There are three (3) different departments issuing permits or licenses of specific types. The proposer will be required to develop requirements and provide a solution that meets the needs of all three (3) departments.

2. Perform an evaluation of the current systems and their capabilities.

3. Design a process flow that eliminates duplicative efforts.

4. Design a system with appropriate interfaces that results in a central repository of relevant permit information.

5. Propose the software with necessary capabilities and provide the licensing to implement the system. A copy of the software license requiring execution shall be submitted with the proposal. The City will consider a hosted solution as well.

6. Provide project management services for the implementation of the system. Project management activities shall include but not be limited to implementation plan, communication plan, schedule for implementation and rollout, progress reports, issues log and documented resolutions to issues, and training plan.

7. Provide on-site training and remote training, as appropriate.

8. List tasks or duties (as applicable).

For system implementation projects, it is advantageous to provide as much detail as possible regarding the functional and technical requirements. If an assessment is conducted internally to develop the functional requirements (what you want the system to do), the information should be included in the RFP. This will provide proposers with the information necessary to submit a good proposal. In addition, make sure that your IT department is involved early on. There might be some technical requirements that the organization may have. These may include access or security and other issues. There could be considerations as to whether the system should be web-based or if your IT department prefers to maintain the system in-house. If the latter is the preference, then request the submission of requirements that the organization must meet regarding technology, such as: server capacity, computer equipment, and mobile devices, or other technical capabilities that the agency must have in order to implement the system.

2. Other Requirements: Do not assume that the agency's priorities are obvious. Include any other requirements to which the selected proposer will be required to adhere once it is awarded a contract. This will avoid surprises and misunderstandings in the price and commitments. Much like the RFQ, if the success of the project is dependent on the key personnel, for example, include requirements for any future substitutions of the key personnel.

> **Example:**
>
> *Key Personnel: The Proposer shall identify key personnel for the project as described in the Submittal Requirements Section. Proposer understand that key personnel is an important criterion by which the proposer will be evaluated and selected; therefore, proposer will not have the ability to replace key personnel, unless there are extenuating circumstances. Any substitutions shall require prior written approval by an authorized representative of the City (organization) and the City will not accept personnel whose credentials are not equal to or better than the key personnel for which substitution is sought. The contract entered into with the successful proposer will include a provision that addresses this requirement.*
>
> *Subcontracting: The proposer shall identify any subcontractors. The proposer shall not replace or add subcontractors without the express written approval of the authorized contracting official.*
>
> *Other Agency Requirements or Goals: Include other agency-specific standard goals and requirements, as appropriate. An example might be minority, women, disadvantaged, and/or local goals.*

Process and Selection

Some agencies have a standard evaluation and selection process; however, you should make the necessary adjustments so that the steps are in agreement with the process for the RFP being developed. Depending on the complexity of the project, the steps may differ. The criteria and submittal requirements must be tailored to the scope of services and requirements.

1. Evaluation and Selection Process: Communicating the process that will be conducted will provide transparency to the vendor community. Allow some flexibility in the process to account for the unknown. The option to request clarifications, presentations, best and final offers or not may play to the organization's advantage. In this section, the use of words like "may" and "will" might be to the agency's advantage. Some agencies use the "competitive range" strategy to further narrow down the number of firms that will be evaluated. This may be more common when a high number of proposals are expected. If price is going to be looked at first, the process must reflect that.

> ### Example:
> The CPO or authorized representative will review proposals received and determine responsiveness. A committee led by Procurement and comprised by representatives of various departments will evaluate responsive proposals received in accordance with the evaluation criteria specified for this RFP. The preliminary result may cause the committee to shortlist those proposers that best meet the criteria. Shortlisted proposers may be invited to submit clarifications and/or make a presentation following specific City (agency) requirements. In considering references, the City may seek information and references from projects and organizations that are not expressly listed on the proposal as a reference.
>
> The City (agency) may request best and final offers from all or the shortlisted proposers. The evaluation committee will recommend the proposer that meets the goals of the RFP and the requirements to successfully perform the services at the best price. Best value is determined by balancing the price and the quality of the proposal based on the best interests of the City.
>
> The recommendation will be presented to the Department Head for selection. The selection will be submitted to the CPO for concurrence with the selection. Upon concurrence by the CPO, contract negotiations will be initiated with the

selected proposer. If negotiations are not successful, the City (agency) may terminate negotiations and begin contract negotiations with the next ranked proposer offering the best value.

The final selection and negotiated contract will be submitted to the governing body, as appropriate, for final approval and execution.

2. <u>Evaluation Criteria</u>: In order to simplify the evaluation process once proposals are received, it is recommended to group criteria according to the three steps: responsiveness, qualification and technical requirements, and price. Each of these steps represents a milestone in the process. Dividing the criteria into these three steps will help provide guidance to evaluation committee members. It will avoid confusion as to when to consider the information provided.

When listing the criteria, organize it so as to flow with the order in the evaluation process. That is, since the first step in the evaluation process is the responsiveness test, list it first. For a proposal to be responsive, it must meet all of the requirements necessary for the evaluation team to actually conduct the evaluation in accordance with the criteria. Once the determination of responsiveness is made, proposals deemed responsive move on to the next step in the evaluation. The result of the first step of the example below is a pass or fail outcome.

> **Example Criteria - Responsiveness:** *Does the proposal substantially conform to RFP submission requirements necessary to evaluate the proposal?*
>
> **Scenario:** *The success of the project depends largely on the experience of the key personnel proposed, but a proposer provides no information on key personnel. If the evaluation team were to evaluate the proposal, the team would not be able to rate the key personnel, an essential part of the proposal. If the proposer were to be allowed to correct this major omission, it could be considered an unfair advantage. There is a way to avoid these dilemmas: If the information on which the evaluation committee will make a determination regarding a criterion is missing, then the proposal should be deemed non- responsive.*

Perfect proposals are a rare occurrence. If a proposal is missing information on a form that can be found elsewhere in the proposal, the evaluation committee may still be able to evaluate the proposal. It that case, it may not be a responsiveness issue. Every now and then one encounters a law that requires certain information on a form to be considered responsive. This is not the ideal scenario from the procurement perspective, and any errors or omissions may become a costly mistake for the proposer and ultimately the agency.

Once you separate the responsive proposals from those that are not, the second step is to evaluate all responsive proposals. In the second step, the evaluation committee will measure how well proposers meet the qualifications and requirements stated in the RFP. These are the criteria that were deemed necessary, in the organization's opinion, to select the firm that can successfully perform the services and meet the goals of the agency/organization. This is going to be an essential part of the process; therefore, it is imperative to have criteria that are relevant to the specific scope of services. The procurement professional must make sure that the criteria will help make a determination of the quality of the proposals received and that the documents submitted are relevant by providing the information that is needed to make a decision.

Listing the criteria in order of importance may enhance the flow of the document. In the example below, the assumption is that the first two criteria are critical to the success of the project; therefore, they are listed first. Later in the process, if a proposer fails to receive an acceptable score in the first two, they will not move to a shortlist. This provides a visual hierarchy.

> **Example Criteria:** *Technical or Qualification Requirements - Responsive proposals will be evaluated in accordance with the following criteria:*
>
> a. *Quality of the proposed solution and its ability to meet the functional requirements of departments and the centralized functions.*
>
> b. *Professional qualifications and experience of the team to successfully perform the services described in this RFP.*

c. *Professional qualifications and (specialized) experience of key personnel to successfully perform the services in the role proposed.*

d. *Understanding of the goals and quality of the proposed plan of action including but not limited to schedule, implementation strategy, and training.*

e. *Capacity of the firm to perform the services within the schedule proposed.*

f. *Local availability of key personnel to facilitate implementation.*

g. *Financial stability to successfully undertake the project.*

h. *Ability to meet (list all other agency) requirements.*

Listing these qualitative criteria in descending order of importance will help simplify the evaluation process later. Similar to the RFQ, you may create tiers of criteria to avoid awarding a contract to a proposer that met or scored high in criteria that have less relevance to the potential success of the project. Different agencies have different preferences as to the level of information communicated out to the vendors. The document may indicate if the criteria are listed in descending order of importance, or indicate whether the proposer must achieve a certain rating on the most critical criteria to be considered. That is, if the proposal is to develop and implement a system and the proposer is rated high in all criteria except for the quality of the proposed solution and or qualifications of the firm, will the organization feel comfortable awarding a contract to a firm with questionable credentials or a solution that may not be appropriate to meet the goals stated in the RFP? Discuss the relevance of each criterion with the evaluation committee members and reach agreement prior to RFP issuance. Also, invest the time and effort in the drafting of good, relevant criteria. See Chapter IV for criteria development.

The last step in the RFP process is to consider price, except for any other variations of the process adopted for specific projects. Why is this the last consideration one may ask? Why not consider it along with the qualifications? Well, the price is only relevant if the proposer is deemed to have the credentials and the quality of the proposal is such that the evaluation committee has deemed the proposal qualified to perform the services. The price is not relevant if the proposer does not possess the qualifications to perform the services. Some agencies first look at price to establish a competitive range; however, it is important to have a good and clear scope. Otherwise, the organization might miss some opportunities. A point of consideration is that if price has that much weight, perhaps the method merits reconsideration.

> **Example Criteria: Price Proposal:** Reasonableness of the Price Proposal in comparison to the value offered and relevancy of that value to the agency's requirements.

Again, the price is only relevant if the firm meets the level of qualifications necessary or desired to successfully perform the services. Looking at price after determining who can perform the services with a similar level of success will allow true comparison of value vs. price. This is where you can balance value with price. How do we do this? It depends on the goals of the project and the overall benefit to the agency and taxpayers. There are times when value and price meet at the top, but often the best-qualified firm may be unaffordable to the agency. In the latter situation, the agency must make a decision as to the merits of the proposals and if the additional value is beneficial to the agency. That is, an agency with limited budget may need to decide if a state of the art program is needed and yet run the risk of not being able to maintain the program because the agency is not equipped to do so, or instead go with a proposal that adequately meets the agency's needs.

> **Case Study:** An agency issued an RFP to develop a formal program for contracting with minority and women businesses. The scope of services required the proposer to perform an assessment of the current efforts, recommend enhancements, and develop formal internal procedures for monitoring and reporting. The agency did not have a formal program but had engaged in a series of efforts to respond to the administration's goals. Upon receipt of proposals, the evaluation committee evaluated all responsive proposals. After the evaluation, there was a proposal that stood out in terms of quality of proposal, proposed plan of action, and the experience that the members brought to the table. However, when the price of the shortlisted proposals was considered, the evaluation committee determined that the

price proposed by the highest ranked, while reasonable for the services proposed, significantly exceeded the budget available. When faced with the decision to make a recommendation, the committee referred back to the requirements and the actual scope of the project. The decision was to recommend the next highest qualified proposal at a price that was more affordable to the agency. The second highest ranked proposal also offered high quality and the proposal adhered to the scope of the project. Conversely, the highest qualified proposal offered features that were not part of the scope of services in the RFP, but would have been nice to have if the agency had a mature program. While the highest qualified proposer offered higher expertise, the level of service that the proposer was offering far exceeded what the agency was prepared to support at the time. The additional value came at a price. The agency went forward with the award to the second highest qualified proposer because it offered the balance between value and price. The value added proposed stayed within the agency's budget.

3. Submittal Requirements: It is important to tell the prospective proposers how to submit, what to submit, how many copies, and where to submit the proposal. If there are specific format requirements, my advice is that you provide easy to follow instructions.

a. Format: For the convenience of the evaluation committee, it is best to provide instructions that can help achieve uniformity in the presentation of information. This uniformity will facilitate the search for information during the evaluation process and make the process go more smoothly. In developing those instructions, it's important to be practical. Request the submission of information in a format that your agency can support.

Example:
Format: *Proposer shall submit one hard copy original and _____ copies of proposals on paper 8-½" X 11", single-sided print, and bound on the left side. Paper shall have a minimum of 30% recycled content. Information shall be organized in the order listed below and separated by labeled tabs. Electronic copies shall be submitted in CD ROM (or USB) format. (Indicate the number of soft copy material.) Expensive paper and bindings are discouraged as the*

agency will not return proposals nor will it compensate the proposer for any expenses associated with proposer's participation in this process.

b. <u>Content</u>: As discussed earlier, the submittal requirements must be in sync with the evaluation criteria. These are the documents and information that the evaluation committee will be reviewing to determine if the proposals received are deemed to have met all relevant requirements, are qualified to perform the services, and have submitted a reasonable price. It corresponds to the documents required to make a determination at each step in the evaluation. That is, if you are evaluating the qualifications of the firms for a specific project, you need information on the firm such as experience in projects relevant to the one for which you are seeking proposals.

<u>Important Note</u>: For purposes of illustration, the submittal requirements in the example below are synced with the evaluation criteria in the example provided under the criteria section. The actual submittal requirements will vary depending on the project scope. This is similar to the hiring process, where résumé, writing samples, transcripts, and references are required, and where a candidate is evaluated for a specific position. Likewise, when submitting a proposal, the information that is required to evaluate a firm's qualifications depends on the scope of services and the criteria that will be used to determine if the proposer is qualified to perform such services. For the purpose of illustrating the relevance of the submittal requirements, when one compares the requirements to apply for a passport and that of applying for a job, we can easily see that the submission requirements are different. The goals of going through the process are different. This is what happens with RFP submissions. The purpose and the expected outcome have a direct relation to the information that is required and how the information is processed or evaluated.

Some of the submittal requirements may not link directly to a particular criterion, but may be necessary to establish the validity of the proposal. An example of this is the cover letter and certain agency-specific forms.

The cover letter may help you establish the validity of the proposal. Some organizations may require an ink signature. In the cover letter, you may want to know if the person submitting the proposal is an authorized representative of the team and if he/she is authorized to bind the company or team to the commitments made in proposal in the event that it is ultimately accepted by the agency/organization. You may require in the cover letter an express commitment to provide the services as proposed. The letter may also provide information to help you establish a list of proposers, team members, and contacts. Having this information summarized and handy is helpful throughout the procurement process. The proposer will generally include a transmittal letter with the proposal; why not make it work to your benefit?

The executive summary is extremely helpful, especially on large projects. Executive summaries can provide the high level information that may be needed throughout the process.

> **Example:**
> **Cover Letter.** *The cover letter shall indicate the names of the firms comprising the team, the name and contact information of the lead person, and a statement committing to provide the services as proposed with the key personnel identified. The letter shall also state that its author or signatory is an authorized representative of the team.*
>
> *2)* **Executive Summary:** *Submit a brief executive summary. It shall include the Proposer's understanding of the goals and a summary of the proposed approach or strategy. Describe why and how the team is qualified to provide the services by providing a brief summary of the experience of the firms (prime and subcontractors). If team members have worked together in other projects, please provide the name of the project(s).*

When requesting qualification information, be specific. Do not leave the requirement open to interpretation. You may end up with very different information for each of the proposals, which may require extensive clarifications. When developing the submittal requirements, refer often to the criteria to make sure that you are asking for the information and documents necessary to evaluate the proposal on each criterion.

> **Example-cont.:**
> *3)* **Proposed software/technology:** *Describe the software proposed for the project and any specific requirements of*

implementing the software to meet the agency's needs. Proposer shall indicate why this software is being recommended. Attach copy of the software license agreement, as appropriate. Note: The agency may request demonstrations of the software capabilities. If a hosted solution is proposed, proposer shall provide any information associated with the service offered including but not limited to data access, ownership, and how the data will be transitioned to the agency should the contract come to an end.

4) **Qualifications of the Firms:** Provide a brief description of the firm(s). Please submit a list of relevant projects. Include the name of the project, a brief description, the dollar value, date of performance, and contact information (name, title, organization, phone number, and email address).

5) **Qualifications of Key Personnel.** Submit chronological resumes for each key personnel. Provide a list of projects in which key personnel performed in a similar role to that proposed. Reference information shall include the project name, name of the organization, contact person (name, title, phone number, and email address), a brief description of the project, the dollar value, and the role performed.

6) **Action Plan.** Provide a project plan for implementation, including but not limited to assessment of current state; development of detailed functional requirements and technical requirements; description of the methodology for implementation and project management; outline of stakeholder communication plan and stakeholder engagement; and training methodology indicating the number of hours included in the proposal for training, and training materials.

Attach a proposed schedule depicting key milestones and any critical path items, as appropriate.

Provide an organization chart depicting the name, role of each key personnel, and the firm. If there are subcontractors or firms partnering, include the role of each firm and identify the key personnel employer.

7) **Teams Capacity:** Provide a chart of key personnel and their availability for the project particularly during the time of their proposed involvement in the project. Include

information on level of commitment to other projects and the expected date of completion for such commitments.

8) **Local Availability of Key Personnel:** Provide a list of key personnel that will be locally available during the performance of the project. Indicate if proposer anticipates key personnel relocations and/or indicate travel frequency of key personnel proposed.

9) **Financial Stability:** Provide a copy of audited statements for the last three fiscal years. Include, at a minimum, the balance sheet, corresponding notes, and related schedules, such as income/loss statements.

10) **Other Requirements:** Add other agency or project-specific requirements as appropriate.

The price proposal is a submittal requirement, but it is considered after the qualifications. To avoid the temptation of reviewing price with qualifications, it's best to require proposers to submit pricing in a separate sealed envelope. Remember, there is no point in spending the time to review price if the firm cannot demonstrate that it can do the job.

Example – cont. –
11) **Price Proposal:** Submit a price proposal detailed in accordance with the attached format. Include the itemization for consulting fees, estimated reimbursable expenses, software license and/or hosting expenses. Indicate the level of effort in terms of number of hours, hourly rates, any hosting subscription fees or software payments required. The training price shall be itemized as follows: face-to-face training, online training, and training materials. Specify the price to provide support during and after the implementation. (Depending on the project, additional information may be necessary.) Also, include a list of expenses for which proposer expects reimbursement.

c. Place and Deadline for Submission: Accuracy is extremely important in this section; therefore, please double and triple check to make sure that you are providing the correct information. Dates often change from the first draft; therefore, I advise to always check this section carefully. Ask a coworker to review it for you. Many agencies provide this information on the cover page of the RFP. That's ideal; however, if you decide to duplicate the information, it is crucial that no discrepancies occur. This part of the RFP should indicate the date, time, location for RFP submission, and identification information, such as: the title of the RFP, name of the proposer, the date and time for the pre-proposal conference, and any other information that the agency may deem relevant.

Example:

Proposals shall be submitted no later than _____ on _____. Late proposals will/shall (depends on your agency's policy) not be accepted after the date and time of the specified herein.

Proposals shall be delivered to:

Procurement Number

Name of Agency

Submitted to the attention of:

Physical address where the Proposal shall be delivered

Pre-Proposal Conference: (date, time, location)

Deadline for the submission of questions:

Submit any questions in writing to _____ via email no later than the deadline for questions indicated above.

The (agency) may issue addenda or clarifications prior to the due date and time for the RFP submission. In order to receive notifications, each prospective proposer must register on the (agency's) website. Failure to register will prevent the prospective proposer from receiving addenda or clarifications issued for this RFP.

If delivery is made by courier service, the Proposal must be received at the correct location by the time and date specified. It is the responsibility of the Proposer to see that the delivery is made as required in this RFP.

Include a note to disclaim responsibility for receipt of proposals when a pro-poser elects to submit it via courier service. It is not unusual for a proposer to hire a third party to deliver the proposal to the agency. Since there is a risk of late submission, protect the agency from late submission issues in the event that the courier service delivers the package to the wrong place.

Exhibits and Forms

Add any exhibits related to the RFP scope first, then any boilerplate or forms that all vendors are expected to complete or execute. Whenever possible, include a draft of the contract that the selected proposer will be expected to sign. This will facilitate contract negotiations later on and will allow the agency to evaluate the exceptions taken to any of the agency's terms and conditions. Some organizations include a criterion to formally evaluate and consider exceptions taken by vendors on the standard contracts. This will help determine if entering into negotiations with a vendor will run into major hurdles in the negotiations, which could delay the award of the contract and implementation of the project. There is a cost to all parties involved associated with extended negotiations; therefore, some agencies do consider this as a factor in the selection process.

RFP EVALUATION PROCESS

As it was stated before, the purpose of the RFP is to select the firm that can provide the best value by balancing the qualifications with the price.

To review the process, first all proposals go through the responsiveness review. This is a pass or fail step. Only responsive proposals move on to the evaluation of qualifications and technical proposal.

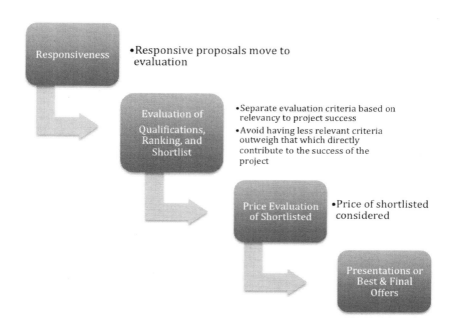

Responsiveness
• Responsive proposals move to evaluation

Evaluation of Qualifications, Ranking, and Shortlist
• Separate evaluation criteria based on relevancy to project success
• Avoid having less relevant criteria outweigh that which directly contribute to the success of the project

Price Evaluation of Shortlisted
• Price of shortlisted considered

Presentations or Best & Final Offers

The second step in the evaluation process can make or break the project. The result of this step may translate into a contract to a proposer; therefore, it is essential that this step be conducted with strict adherence to the process and criteria specified in the RFP. I cannot emphasize enough the importance of weighing criteria appropriately, as it will impact the final result of the process. There are criteria that are considered critical to the success of the project and more emphasis is given as we review the proposals. There is a second type of criteria that, while important, any ambiguities can be corrected through clarifications or as the full scope of the project and circumstances are revealed. The third type of criteria is that where compliance is required and corrections can be done administratively through further conversations or minor form corrections.

This third type of criteria requires some clarification. It does not mean that the vendor gets a second bite at the apple. It is a practical approach to deal with certain requirements that while worthwhile, it makes procurement an almost impossible task for both the agency and the vendors. I know of an agency that was required to include a form with every procurement document. The form required that the vendor select one of the options. With little to no time to introduce the form and educate vendors, procurement officials were directed to reject any vendor submission where the form was not included or if the vendor failed to make a selection on the form correctly. The effort to redo the procurement each time due to the number of rejected proposals garner enough attention to relax the requirement to a more practical level. Likewise, there are certain forms that are required and yet it may be difficult for vendors to get it right. As I mentioned in Chapter II, the submission of ownership information may be one of those forms. It is especially difficult to get a perfect submission when ownership is several layers deep. In categorizing criteria, it is important to consider the impact to the project so as not to include in this category the qualification factors that are key to the overall success of the project.

The objective of the technical and qualifications evaluation is sometimes challenged by the structure of the evaluation process. Whether the preference is qualitative or quantitative evaluation, the concern is the same: Will less relevant criteria outweigh other criteria that can ultimately make or break the project? If you choose a numeric approach, test possible scenarios including extreme scenarios before finalizing the RFP. Absent the testing of all possible scenarios prior to finalizing the evaluation process, it may be much simpler to establish tiers of criteria. That is, a firm that has not at least met the criteria that is the most relevant or critical to the success of a project should not make it to the shortlist. I have seen many occasions where the firm that has scored the highest had questionable qualifications on the criteria that matter most. When this happens, it is at times difficult to justify recommending a team that ended up lower in the ranking because of the disproportionate weight established for the criteria upfront. Many using the numeric approach simply establish weights or percentages of the total score. This may or may not work, unless the approach is more scientifically developed so as to always have the right result. Of course, that will take significant testing. There are systems available in the market, but the scoring is as good as the initial set up.

As a rule of thumb, if it is important enough to make it as a criterion, the rating received for that criterion should have some impact in the selection of a proposer. The relevance may get lost when the scores are totaled or averaged, and a poor score may be offset by a higher score elsewhere. This approach may essentially eliminate the relevance of an individual criterion. When developing the evaluation instructions and scoring or rating process, it's important to keep in mind the relevance of each criterion. If the same weight is applied and the process calls for simply adding the results for each criterion or even averaging the scores of all evaluators, the result may not be desirable, as it may not reflect the quality of the proposals accurately. It is, therefore, that I make the recommendations below:

1. **Separate Criteria by Level of Importance.** Categorize the criteria by determining their relative value and relevancy to the success of the project.

2. **Make each criterion count.** If a criterion is critical to the success of the project, do not shortlist submittals that do not at least receive an acceptable rating or score in that criterion.

3. **Assign qualitative value to numeric scores.** If you elect to use numeric scoring, define what it means to receive a specific score. This will allow you to translate a score into a qualitative explanation and differentiate results particularly when the difference comes down to one or two points.

4. **Prepare to deal with substandard scores.** Develop short guidelines on how to rank proposals and how to deal with poor scores or ratings.

5. **Keep a list of strengths and weaknesses.** Require the evaluation team members to justify the rating or score focusing on strengths and weaknesses. This will help reduce subjectivity in the process. The comments (strengths and weaknesses) that the evaluation team members provide will help you construct an evaluation summary and the basis for the recommendation. This summary will help support the selection and no additional work will be required to conduct debriefings with unsuccessful proposers later on. It's much easier to collect these comments as the evaluation progresses than to have to go back to evaluation team members and request the information.

6. **Determine the real cost of the proposal to the agency.** Evaluating price is more than simply looking at the bottom line or even the fixed price. Some agencies go through the exercise of evaluating the total cost of ownership. It is important to at least understand the total cost to the organization. Sure, there is the fully loaded price to purchase the services, but to understand the total cost to the agency it is important to factor into the project cost the internal expense associated with implementing the project. That is, any

necessary computer upgrades, staff time devoted to the project implementation, any staff augmentation to help support the workload, any additional equipment for the additional staff, space needed and office expenses, and others as may be deemed necessary. This process, of course, may have been part of the budgeting process before going out to solicit proposals for project implementation. If that upfront analysis has occurred, then the analysis should be simpler.

Again, I have implemented these recommendations for at least 20 years and have successfully been able to provide solid backup to the results of the evaluation process. When the results were challenged in court, the process served to further validate the results. It may seem simpler to throw some scores and add them up, but in the end having to go back and justify the scores is much more time consuming for those involved.

SUMMARY

When drafting an RFP, first try to understand what the end user is seeking, do your best to clearly articulate the requirements in the document, organize the document in a logical manner so that information is easy to follow, and keep the end in mind. Ask the end users, what, in their view, a successful process will produce and what will be needed to achieve that result. Your approach will make the difference between the robotic process of feeding information into a standard document and the critical thinking that you bring to the table as the procurement professional.

CHAPTER IV
Alignment & Consistency

ACHIEVING ALIGNMENT

As it was discussed for each of the basic procurement methods, there are four areas that need to be aligned so that the procurement results in the selection of a firm(s) or team that can successfully deliver the goods or provide the services identified in the solicitation document, particularly in RFQs and RFPs. These areas are: goals, scope, criteria, and submittal requirements. It's important to understand the goals of the procurement or project to then develop a scope of services that expands on the desired result and helps to achieve the goals of the project. In the RFQ or RFP, the scope of services is less prescriptive than in a bid document. In the RFP situation, the agency is seeking a solution or services not readily available within the agency.

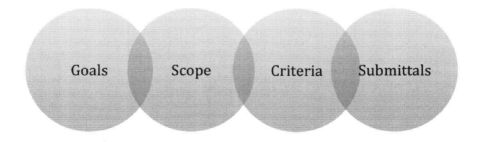

Goals   Scope   Criteria   Submittals

In these two methods of procurement, the criteria are developed as a way of identifying the characteristics or attributes that are relevant for a firm/team to be successful in the project implementation. These are the characteristics on which vendors will be judged to determine if the firm(s) possesses those qualifications or attributes to successfully perform the services required. The submittal requirements are the documents or information that will help evaluation team members make that judgment and ultimately identify the firm or team that possesses the attributes or qualifications sought to ultimately achieve success in the implementation of the project.

CONSISTENT TERMINOLOGY

Say what you mean and mean what you say! Consistency in the use of terminology will avoid confusion in the process. Although some procurement professionals use some of the terminology interchangeably, doing so often creates confusion to those less experienced leading to myths and misconceptions of the process. For example, when proposals are labeled as bids, does it mean that the selection is based on the lowest price or best value? How do we keep end users from getting confused about how price is weighted in each instance? For the sake of clarity, I recommend that you use terminology consistently.

Bid Method

Bid – The document submitted by the bidder in response to an invitation to bid.

Bidder – The firm responding to an invitation to bid by submitting a bid.

Invitation for Bid or Invitation to Bid – The solicitation document prepared by the organization (generally the procurement professional) and issued to invite businesses to submit a bid to provide the goods or services specified.

Request for Qualifications Method

Responses or Submittal – The actual response document or statement of qualifications submitted by a respondent as a result of the RFQ.

Respondent – The firm or team responding to the RFQ by submitting qualifications in accordance with the instructions provided in the RFQ.

Request for Qualifications – The solicitation document issued by an organization to invite businesses to submit their qualifications for a specific purpose.

Request for Proposals Method

Proposals – The actual response submitted by the Proposer in response to the RFP issued by an organization.

Proposer – The firm or team that submits a proposal in response to the RFP.

Request for Proposals – The solicitation document issued by an organization for the purpose of inviting businesses to submit proposals for a specific project or program.

STANDARDIZATION

There may be more opportunities to standardize bid documents given their prescriptive nature. When standardizing the RFQ or RFP documents, I advise allowing for some flexibility to accommodate the diverse nature of projects. One-size fits all approach can further complicate the procurement, as it will create confusion at the evaluation stage. It is more advantageous to provide focus to the standardization. That is, within the different categories of spend or type of procurement, standardization makes more sense. By type of procurement I am referring to whether it is work, professional services, commodities, supplies, or equipment. The different standard documents may be confusing if the staff consists of people known to be "jacks of all trades" instead of category managers specializing in one or a handful of areas. It is, therefore, important to be practical and determine what makes sense for the organization based on its operations and staffing capabilities. Even when organizations standardize processes and documents, the standardization should not sacrifice the effectiveness of the procurement method.

SAMPLE RFQ AND RFP OUTLINE
Title Page: Agency Name, Title, Procurement Contact and Contact Information, Due date & Time, Pre-Submittal or Pre-Proposal Conference date, time, and location.

Purpose: One or two sentences generally expanding the on the procurement title.

Background: A paragraph or two about the organization. Generally available on the agency's website. This can be standardized.

Problem Statement and/or Goals: Statement of why the agency needs the services and what the agency is seeking to accomplish by contracting for the services.

Scope of Services: Provide a list of tasks, responsibilities, and information about the project requirements.

Requirements: List any agency requirements that proposer/ respondent will need to meet if awarded a contract.

Evaluation and Selection Process: Describe the process that will be followed to evaluate responses to the RFQ or RFP. The language can be semi-standardized and tailored to the project.

Evaluation Criteria: Develop criteria directly related to the scope of services and the goals of the project. Some level of standardization is feasible, but customization to the project is crucial and the order in which the criteria are listed is important.

Submittal Requirements

> *Format: Provide specific instructions on how the submission needs to be organized and presented. This language can be standardized.*

> *Content: The content needs to be customized to the project and the criteria. Some standardization is possible within project categories (i.e. engineering, IT, HR, planning, and others).*

> *Date, Time & Place for Submission: Provide specific instructions on where to submit and deadline for submission. Also, include information on how the envelope should be labeled when submitted to the agency. This information must be consistent with the information on the cover page.*

Exhibits and Attachments: Include any procurement-specific attachments, exhibits, or formats. Also, include any standard information that the agency requires with all procurements.

NOTE: The variations of specific titles used for each section is up to the agency or procurement professional. The content of the document and a logical flow of information are more important.

CRITERIA AND SUBMITTAL REQUIREMENTS ALIGNMENT

Responsiveness and responsibility are critical elements of the process, including the bid process. Again, responsiveness refers to the actual submission, while responsibility refers to the firm submitting the response to the procurement. Since responsiveness is a legal matter, procurement professionals should not make this decision without consulting upper management and sometimes your legal department. Before communicating that a response is deemed non-responsive, check with your manager. You may need your manager's approval and/or support if your opinion is challenged.

When drafting qualitative criteria in an RFQ or RFP, make sure that you put the criteria in the context of the scope of services. A firm or person may have excellent credentials overall, but those credentials may not be relevant to a specific project. Developing clear and concise criteria that will be used to measure quality will avoid confusion in the evaluation stage.

The importance of the criteria cannot be emphasized enough. This section deserves thoughtful attention, as this means a business opportunity to a vendor and the success of the project rides on the evaluation made by the evaluation committee. This is an opportunity to add value to the process as procurement professional. The chart below shows some examples of criteria dos and don'ts.

DRAFTING CRITERIA	
Do	**Don't**
Qualifications and experience of the team as evidenced by relevant experience in similar projects.	Qualifications of the Team
Qualifications and specialized experience of the key personnel to perform the services for the role proposed as evidenced by relevant experience.	Résumés
Quality of the proposed plan of action and its ability to meet the project goals.	Executive Summary and Project Plan
Reasonableness of Price Proposal in relation to value proposed.	Price proposal

Evaluation Criteria ≠ Submittal Requirements

Resist the temptation to merge evaluation criteria with submittal requirements. These need to be in sync, but they serve a different purpose.

The evaluation criteria are the specific attributes that will be considered to determine if the proposer or respondent is qualified to perform the services and the level of quality offered. The criteria establish context for the consideration of those attributes or qualifications offered by the proposer to determine whether they are relevant to a specific project or purpose as stated in the solicitation document. That is, while a proposer's qualifications may be impressive without a specific context, those qualifications may not be relevant to the project for which consideration is being given. The criteria define the shape of the piece of the puzzle that would fit the picture. The criteria sets the standard for relevancy as it relates to the project. This is where the analytical skills of the procurement professional add value to the RFP. The procurement professional, in coordination with the end user, can help extract the key areas for consideration as they relate to the vendor's qualifications and thereby help the evaluation committee recommend a firm that is poised to deliver quality services and successfully complete the project.

The submittal requirements section, on the other hand, represents a detailed list of documents and information that the committee will review to make the assessment in accordance with the evaluation criteria. I advise that you request only information that is useful to the evaluation committee and that will ultimately be considered. Often agencies have a standard list of information that is not needed for the evaluation and tends to complicate the review process.

As stated before, attempting to merge evaluation criteria and submittal requirements tends to create confusion and restrict the review of information to make a determination on the rating of a proposer or a specific criterion. Also, when the submittal requirements have very little connection with the criteria, the evaluators are left wondering how to come to a rating for a specific criterion. Simplicity is the best approach. The chart below depicts the criteria with corresponding submittal requirement.

Note: In the example above, not all submittal requirements are included. The goal is to illustrate the relationship between the qualitative criteria and the corresponding submittal requirement. Also, notice that the word "please" is not used in the submittal requirements in the example above. The use of the word "please" in this instance may give the impression that the submission of the information requested is optional.

Example – RFP Criteria and Submittal Requirements

RELATIONSHIP BETWEEN CRITERIA AND SUBMITTAL REQUIREMENTS	
Sample Criteria (Sets the Standard)	Sample Submittal Requirement (Specific information needed)
1. Qualifications of the firm/team to successfully perform the project as evidenced by its experience in comparable projects performed, preferably of similar magnitude to the project described in this RFP.	1. Provide a brief summary of the firm's experience and qualifications. Include a list of at least three projects of similar scope performed in the last five (5) years. For each project, include the name of the project, organization, contact information (name, title, phone number, and email address), a brief description of the project, the duration, date completed, and the dollar value. If a team of firms is proposed, indicate which of the team members participated in the projects listed. If any of the key personnel participated in one or more of the projects listed, list names and roles. If the proposer is comprised of a team of firms, indicate if any of the firms worked together on any of the projects listed.

2. Qualifications and specialized experience of key personnel as evidenced by comparable experience performing services similar to the role proposed.	2. Provide chronological resumes of key personnel. Include a list of three to five projects where the key personnel performed in a similar role to that proposed. Provide the following information: description and title of the project, reference contact information (name, title, email, and phone number), the dollar value of the project, date of completion, and description of the role performed.
3. Quality of the proposed project plan and capacity of the team to successfully complete the project.	3. Provide a description of the project strategy for implementation to successfully meet the goals of the project. The Plan shall include but not be limited to project management plan, communication plan, documentation to be produced, reports, training, and support. Attach a proposed project schedule depicting key milestones. Also, include the organization chart depicting the name of the key personnel, role and employer (if team of firms).
4. Local availability of the key personnel and the ability of the Proposer to respond to project demands without causing project delays.	4. List all key personnel that are or will be locally available. Indicate if any key personnel will require relocation and/or frequent travel throughout the duration of their involvement in the project. Also, include information on the areas of the project that do not require local presence and those backup personnel that are local and will be available to assist as needed.
5. Capacity of the key personnel to provide the services within the schedule proposed based on other project commitments.	5. Provide a key personnel capacity chart indicating level of commitment to this project and the time that each key personnel is committed to other projects. Provide the expected date of completion for other commitments.
6. Financial stability of the proposer to successfully undertake the project.	6. Provide audited financial statements for the last three years. Include auditor's letter of opinion, balance sheet, notes, and related schedules. The City may consider unaudited financial statements provided that Proposer is able to demonstrate its financial capacity to successfully undertake the project and achieve timely completion.
7. Level and quality of compliance with the goals of the Disadvantaged Business Enterprise Program (DBE).	7. Provide the level of commitment for each certified DBE firm, the role proposed for each firm, and any key personnel. Provide the information required in items 1 and 2 for each firm.
Price Proposal Reasonableness of the price proposal in comparison to the value offered.	8. Provide the price proposal in a separate sealed envelope, in the format provided and itemizing components listed. Provide itemization for consulting fees and reimbursable expenses estimated. Indicate the level of effort in terms of number of hours, hourly rates, and profit. (Depending on the project and funding source, information required may be modified.)

HIGH LEVEL VIEW OF EVALUATIONS

Finally, if you understand the considerations of each of the methods, it will be easier to understand the variations that exist for the basic methods described herein.

Quick Reference Guide

Method	Objective	Generally Appropriate for	Considerations		
			Responsiveness	Qualifications	Price
Bid	Lowest responsive & responsible Bidder	Supplies, equipment, commodities, work services, construction	First Step	Third step for the apparent lowest bidder only.	Second step for all responsive bidders
RFQ	Best Qualified	Architectural and engineering services Certain professional services as legally required Pre-Qualification	First Step	Second step for all responsive respondents. Consider the level of importance of each criterion and factor in its weight in the overall evaluation.	Not Considered
RFP	Best Value Balance between best qualifications and price	Seeking a solution to a problem. Price consideration not legally prohibited. Certain complex combination of services, equipment, goods, or general services	First Step	Second step for all responsive proposers. Consider the level of importance of each criterion and factor in its weight in the overall evaluation.	Third step for qualified or shortlisted proposers

CONCLUSION

There are at least four things that the procurement professional should understand when selecting the right competitive procurement method. First, the right method adds efficiency to the organization. The selection of the method is not "the flavor of the day" type of choice. The selection of the method is directly related to the goals of the project and how to more effectively achieve those goals. In selecting the method, one should start by considering the simplest approach. It will save time and frustration of those involved.

Second, understand the logic of the method's components and how they contribute to the success of the process and more importantly how they contribute to the project's success. A well-constructed solicitation document facilitates the evaluation and selection process as well.

Third, do not overuse standardization. Standard documents save time and effort, provided that the standard language is relevant to the goals and project. Irrelevant standard language tends to increase the complexity of the procurement process and adversely impact clarity.

Last, using terminology consistently helps not only to reduce process confusion, but also to educate those that are sporadically involved in the procurement process.

The value that procurement adds to the process originates in part from the knowledge that the procurement professional brings to table. Possessing a good understanding of the process and how the information needs to fit together in the procurement document is half the battle. Maintaining focus on the goals of the procurement will help deliver vendor recommendations that are more aligned with the goals of the project. As far as the expertise in agency-specific process or even the procurement category: that is expertise acquired over time. It is an accumulation of research and experience. You are contributing your expertise in the process by leading your end user and evaluation team members through a process that may be comparable to a maze at times. You are the procurement process expert with an opportunity to lead and build a team handed to you with every procurement. How cool is that! Go ahead, lead the way to successful procurements and help make the world a better place.

AFTERWORD

When I set out to write this book, I used my own experience and the material that I developed at one time or another to train staff. I put together the book that I would have liked to have then to provide to my team. It would have saved me many hours of work recreating reference material and PowerPoint presentations. I included advice and examples that do not generally make it into the agency's internal procedures manual.

As time goes on, more and more procurement professionals will be exiting the profession taking with them the knowledge that they have accumulated throughout their active years in the profession. While it may not be possible to transfer the experience acquired, primarily because it may take just as much time to transfer years of experience, it is important to transfer the essence of the knowledge derived from the experience. If we can transfer the knowledge on why we choose one method over other, how the parts of the procurement document work together to facilitate the process, and sprinkle some effective techniques learned along the way, I believe that we have done our job. What remains is the application of the concepts, which will need to be tailored to the individual procurement anyway and will require practice to perfect the skills.

While this book is written primarily based on public procurement experience, procurement methods have global application. In talking with colleagues in the private sector and leaders seeking to improve their procurement operations, I have received confirmation that we are all after similar goals: cost savings, efficiencies, value-added interaction, customer-focused approach, creativity, and best practices. The difference is the purpose for achieving the goals. Whether it is improving the bottom line, the market share, or stretching the taxpayers' dollars to provide additional or higher quality services, all organizations can benefit from having a high performing procurement team seeking to stretch the organization's resources.